If I Only Had **Five** Minutes

The Last Will and Testament of a Hip Hop Poet

Tia DeShay

authorHOUSE®

AuthorHouse™
1663 Liberty Drive
Bloomington, IN 47403
www.authorhouse.com
Phone: 1-800-839-8640

First published by AuthorHouse 02/23/2011

ISBN: 978-1-4567-3148-9 (sc)
ISBN: 978-1-4567-3147-2 (e)

Library of Congress Control Number: 2011901712

Printed in the United States of America

Any people depicted in stock imagery provided by Thinkstock are models, and such images are being used for illustrative purposes only. Certain stock imagery © Thinkstock.

This book is printed on acid-free paper.

If You Only Had Five More Minutes
Essie Mae Lockett
(1953 – 2009)

"Hip hop is suppose to uplift and create, to educate people on a larger level and to make a change." - Doug E. Fresh

"I don't create poetry. I create myself, for me my poems are a way to me." — Edith Sodergran

Prelude

I was born in Detroit, Michigan. In 1990, at the age of fifteen, I experienced my first teenage love affair. His name was Hip Hop. Hip Hop and I met through a socially conscious rap group, X Clan. Their album, "To the East, Blackwards" was the first poem Hip Hop wrote to me. I carried it around in my pink boom box and listened to it whenever my parents were not around. Hip Hop's game was flawless. I was hooked.

Our rendezvous included early morning affairs with Rob Base's video "It Takes Two" before I attended classes at Cass Technical High School. Eventually, my parents accepted our relationship. From that point, Hip Hop introduced me to his friends: Salt – n – Pepa, Whodini, Beastie Boys, JJ Fad, Heavy D. and the Boyz, The Fresh Prince and DJ Jazzy Jeff, and the Fat Boys. I loved the way Hip Hop used language to create a space on notebooks and on wax where words were raw, uncensored, thought provoking, and street smart. Hip Hop was Pavlow and I was his test subject.

After leaving home at the age of seventeen, my affair with Hip Hop became more explicit, illicit, dangerous, and self-destructive. He started calling me out my name and abusing my airwaves. But I was too far gone to let go. Our relationship hit a turning point when his man, Tupac Shakur was murdered in 1996 when I was an undergraduate at Eastern Michigan University.

Shakur's death revealed a side of Hip Hop, that before Shakur's death, my mind was not prepared to comprehend. But, in 1996, I understood that Hip Hop, like most men, when taken out of their context, detached from their roots, were not only controversial, but inherently dangerous, and potentially lethal.

My relationship with Hip Hop lasted beyond EMU. Hip Hop was there when I graduated from Wayne State University in 2003 and during my ten year career as an English Teacher and Journalism and Yearbook Adviser for the Detroit Public Schools.

Yeah, our relationship was tumultuous, but it was the new millennium and Hip Hop was going to *Get Rich or Die Tryin*. So while he was catching cases in his pursuit of riches, it was nothing to post his 50 Cent bail because I was his ride or die chick. Hip Hop and I had come too far. I was not going to leave him in the cold.

Every poem I wrote, Hip Hop was there. He romanced me with similes and metaphors. He fed me imagination for breakfast and cooked me verses for dinner. One night, I guess I had finally made Common sense to Hip Hop because he proposed to me at an Open Mic session. He was tired of the one night stands, he wanted marriage.

You see, Hip Hop had flipped the script. His circle of friends had changed. He now hung with Da Truth, Lecrae, Canton Jones, and Flame. He wanted to do more with his five minutes. He wanted to change lives. So, Hip Hop and I jumped the broom and in 2010, I gave birth to our first child. I named her: ***If I Only Had Five Minutes. The Last Will and Testament of a Hip Hop Poet***.

Playlist

Disc One: Life

Interlude:

"...that's what I'm going to do as an artist, as a rapper...I'm going to show the most graphic details of what I see in my community and hopefully they'll stop it...QUICK! It's like my battle cry to America."
– Tupac Shakur, <u>Legacy</u>

Female Terrorism

- **A poem for my sister across the hall, 'cause somebody wrote a poem for me**

1 out of 3 women will be raped in her lifetime.
1 out of 3 women will be raped in her lifetime.

Every 2 seconds a woman will be raped in the U.S.
Every 2 seconds a woman will be raped in the U.S.

Menstrual cycles must be validation for cerebral blood clots
and 1 a.m. nose bleeds.
Preferred on her knees while you force-feed
her your thickness.
Letting her parched lips swallow your existence
her form of repentance
for

dinner being served late
that equated to 3 a.m. 911
state your emergency
Slut
Skank
phone calls.

Ooh let Daddy
Break it down
Break it down
Break it down
Break you down
Break you down
Break you down
into locker room male conquest
reliving how you banged the mess out of her clitoris
How you hit that, split that,
bent that 69 ways

until you came
and covered her with your self-hatred.
Hooked and baited her G-spot
for fleshly payment
of being too full of herself.

So you crucify her
dominatrix style
her butter pecan thighs
spread wide as she rides
your thickness.
Letting her parched lips swallow your existence
her form of repentance
for being

1 out of 3 women raped in her lifetime.
For being 1 out of 3 women raped in her lifetime.
Her love blind
femininity misguided
'cause no one ever told her
she was most high
that she had to feel good on the inside
before he feels good on the outside.

Is it a crime to beat me or isn't it?
Is it a crime to beat me or isn't it?
Is it a crime to beat me or isn't it?
My brothers and sisters
we've gone too long
without asking the question
that we've forgot the answer.
Meanwhile,

Every 2 seconds a woman will be raped in the U.S.
Every 2 seconds a woman will be raped in the U.S.

8.15.2002

Conversate to Elevate

Have you heard?
Sam is dead.
Wait, maybe ya'll didn't hear me,
My man Sam is dead.
You see my man told me
Yada, Yada, Yada and Blahza Splee.
And my man told me
Yaketty, Yaketty, Yak, Yak, Yak
that his homeboy stabbed him in the back.
But my man told me
Yaketty, Yaketty, Yak, Yak, Yak.

Have you heard?
Sam is dead.
Based on he said, she said
bled
at the hand of his own brother
his Roll Dog
for figures
colored green with envy.
Blinded like Stevie
for the love of
show me the money.
Funny
how the game's played
how Sam did not pass go, did not collect his 40 acres and a
mule.

Now society's lost a future father, a soul brother, a warrior.
Beautiful.
Black on purpose.

Too bad this thing called life
is not a dress rehearsal

somebody yellin' cut on an animated set where the wounds
in Sam's back
will win an Emmy for Best Make-Up in a Drama Series
entitled,
"The Projects."
Reality check: Sam is dead.

Another brother lost,
Another mother weeps,
Another child left unborn,
Another sister scorned,
Another generation lost,
Another number,
Another statistic,
Another jail sentence,
Another baby boy,

Pimped and crucified
For 30 pieces of platinum.

Bling bling
Things Fall Apart
when we refuse to start embracing each other, loving each
other, respecting each other, supporting each other,

Instead of killing each other,
Hating each other, lying to each other.

My little soul brother Sam is dead.
And all cats can do and say
And all cats can do and say
And all cats can do and say
Is Yada, Yada, Yada, and Blahza Splee.

10.17.2002

I Carry the Cross

- **dedicated to all my ghetto girls. We won't heal as women until we see ourselves in you.**

Abortions are my ghetto girls' baptism
hoping to be washed clean of the scent of mommy's
boyfriend
whose tongue plays hide and seek in places beyond the
reach of themselves.
So, they sell themselves to little
chocolate boys who learned their ABCs while on parole from
the penitentiary
hoping that they will wash them clean of this concrete jungle
insanity
project mentality
all because he rocks a platinum crucifix that lynches his
spirit.
But she has nowhere else to turn because we have turned
our backs on her
arrogant in our ignorance
denying that we gave birth to her
that we hate her
that we are bitter because of her;
and if we could, we would have aborted her.
But now we are afraid of her
because she reminds us of our illegitimate bastards and our
missed childhoods
and our divorces and the late night dates with Godiva
'cause our husbands
left us for someone that smelled just like her.
And we hide behind MAC lip gloss and shake our heads in
disgust at her
so we erase her existence by blaming Hip Hop
Instead of ourselves.

The shortest distance between 2 points for her is the cradle
to the grave.
Forcing her to lie in a bed made with incestuous sheets.
Don't think you can get rid of her
because I am her
that ghetto girl you try so hard
to forget.
My peoples quiet as it's kept secret.
And I will continue to write her story.

1.27.04

Page 2A

Black pearls reduced to 8th grade copy print on the bottom
of Page 2A.
Black diamonds are no longer forever as our urban jewels
rock themselves to sleep with self - inflicted nooses
muses of journalistic leads.
Writers play Russian Roulette and bet on what's more
newsworthy:
political pride and prejudice or the salvation of our youth.
YouTube and Facebook become mass grave markers for our
youth:
mass media's lost subculture
whose mass funerals are by — lines at the bottom of Page 2A
of yesterday's news
while bruised, inflated egos are our city's state of
emergency.

As our black seeds
bleed black blood and die a black death by black hands
who fear black faces that commit
black on black crimes
whose black hearts
breed black contempt for the black mothers
who birthed them into black holes called ghettos
who grow up to cover themselves with black rage
only to connect the dots of their lives at the bottom of Page
2A.

5.13.08

White Tee

I got death 4 sale
5 for $20
One size fits all.
Here's your once in a lifetime opportunity to be a ghetto
superstar.
All you have to do for your 15 minutes of fame is to be hated
on
by someone that looks just like you
and take 2 to the chest and your life too can be reduced to a
White Tee!

But wait, there's more!
After your life has been the latest fashion statement
your memory will fade after just one spin in the wash cycle.

Why do we pay others to wear our misery on our chests?
It's ridiculous to believe
we've given our children R.I.P. tees
as security blankets instead of hugs.
That our most recent photos of our children are found on the
front of obituaries.
That the only option we give our black boys is 2 check the
boxes labeled: "Dead" or "In Jail."
We've posted more bail
than paid tuition
Yet we wonder why our youth lack ambition.
Maybe if adults did less talking and more listening
maybe if we as a community could turn down the gun shots
and turn up the love songs
maybe we could hear less static
and brothers can stop using funerals to save face
and maybe Mahalia Jackson can give us some of her Amazing
Grace
so that our black boys and black girls can rule the world and
become

what God intended them to be.

3.23.06

Tupac Shakur

All Eyez Were on You
as you spoke about
Changes
through unequivocal means.
You were the ghetto's
dream
White America's
nightmare because you constantly reminded them
that they were the original gangsta's
thugs on Capitol Hill
hiding behind
American Democracy.
You spoke of the ghetto's ills
about the Brenda's Having Babies
and our charcoal colored brothers
Keeping Their Heads Up.
You were the younger generation's Malcolm
who spoke of Unconditional Love
despite being Trapped
in a cycle of systematic fallacies.

How Long Will We Mourn You?
Until it becomes clear
that you exist in all of us
that you are the pendulum
that strikes the balance in the heartz of a ghetto nation.
That you were not imitating life, but a
man reflecting life through the eyes of a political artist.

That you are an ancestor who deserved
a chariot procession from a forgiving people.
May our history books paint your portrait as intimately
and as deserving as your life
reflected.

May it captivate your essence and provide you with
the rendition of accolades that are long overdue.

4.4.99

God's Gift

- **Written for Darryl John Bacon III**

City grime.
Let me disconnect your electricity before you get a chance
to shine.
Bootleg your gift before the world has a chance to unwrap it.
Steal your possibility before you can do the impossible.
Cut you off at the knees before you have a chance to
outgrow me.
Evict your heart after you signed the lease.

But somehow you are still in one peace.

Shatter your looking glass because your reflection was too
much for me to handle.
Stuck my foot out so you could lose your balance.
Guess that's why they call it guilt trippin'.
Rearrange the closet of your life so you could never figure
out what's missing.

But you birthed rivers out of dry places anyway; and took
your ashes and made the hottest color of the season:
Phoenix Rising Red.

With two fish and five loaves five thousand were fed.
Just imagine what ONE will do.
The possibilities are endless.

A nine month seed custom fitted for a time such as this.
Seamless.
Morning in a city of midnight.
A skyscraper in an abandoned city skyline.
Will walk on the Detroit River and invite others to come
with a box of Crayolas and child like imagination.
Will walk the paths of righteousness made out of blue Legos.

Some will yell for him to "Stop!"
God will command him to "Go!"

Eventually he will paint the city Phoenix Rising Red...
Mommy's favorite color.

7.31.2010

Our Grown Woman Selves

As women we are so full of our grown woman selves that we forget that we are the young girls we have grown to despise. We attempt to shake off our organic selves in exchange for silicone injected vagina's that breed botox one night stands on cotton sheets stained with our skin.

We shake ourselves out of our clothing so much so, that when we are fully clothed, men have difficulty comprehending us. So, we dumb down our femininity and cover our breasts with swisher scented lips instead of magnolias. We are shaken but not stirred.

Our behinds are strawberry Jello molds that move on wood grain dance hall floors, swaying themselves as post adolescent legs attempt to balance themselves on Jimmy Choo's swiped clean with American Express subway rides to East Side Detroit. Hoping our designer fig leaves will hide our naked Brown Sugar bodies from melting into his Black Coffee skin that we drink every morning from another sister's coffee mug.

But we're so together that we cook our own love recipe in our cast iron skillets heated by our degrees that we use as oven mitts to protect our hands from feeling our own heartburn. But, we so full of our grown woman selves that we stuff ourselves into plastic wrap so our dresses will fall just right on our suffocated skin that our tongues cannot taste our own honey molasses tears.

But, we continue to paint our lips with pomegranate juice and spray our skin with lavender oil and rosemary to mask the infection that our pecan brown thighs hide, our own self imposed sterilization. Aborting our reflections so that we don't give birth to ourselves.

Instead we still birth each other.

11.27.2010

Despair

Momma Dead.
Daddy Dead.
Dreams Dead.
Trying to incapacitate the voices in my head.
Bled
enough to die 1,000 deaths
life in the fast lane
running on empty
at 100 MPH.
My April Showers
fall on vacant lots
brothers pass another brick on my block
guess that's why they call it a brick wall
that I keep banging my head into.
Searching for love, settling for a make-up bag
that paints a pretty face on a carcass
whose soul was stolen behind yellow "Caution" tape
and crime scene markers.
Whose colors come in Funeral Black
and Graveyard Gray.
Wishing Time could spend the night
and Tomorrow could replace Today
so I could have something to remember
instead of memories of flashing sirens
and newspaper clippings that become Facebook
mementos
and canvasses for oversized white tees
that fade in the spin cycle.

So I recycle the blues
Of Sanchez, Nikki, and Hughes
and find a new color to paint my despair
tagging every brick wall in my hood
'cause I ain't got nothing better to do.
'Cause Momma Dead.

Daddy Dead.
And I've already bled
a 1,000 deaths.

10.19.2010

Disc Two: Love

I'll Always Love Him

His name is Hip Hop.
A global phenomenon.
I heard he got chicks in Italy sprung.
He recites ballads for our
unsung
heroes.
I heard he rocks stages in Rio de Janeiro.
Sometimes he gets caught up in making dinero
but who can deny his Coltrane falsetto.
He rocks inner city ghettos
can pull heart strings like Gepetto
reminds us of inner city blues like Soweto.
A yo sometimes it was hard to watch him grow from B-Boy to
video eye candy
to rockin' mics in Timbos.
He rose
from concrete to international coliseums
he made me understand
the phrase: 'Carpe Diem.'
He's nostalgia
like the original Filas.
I'll always need him.
His sex appeal extends from Amsterdam to New Zealand.

Yeah, I admit
he the reason cats be beefin'
sometimes his lyrics be misleading
changing styles like the seasons.
Yet, he still be makin'
Common sense to me.
I can give you 21 reasons why I love him like 50.
First there's
Biggie
Tupac
Eminem

And Nas
Lauryn Hill
The Fugees
And Camron

EPMD
LL Cool J
Mos Def
And Jay Z
There's NWA
Ice T
And MC Lyte

DJ Jazzy Jeff
and the Fresh Prince
Run D.M.C.
Eve

Please believe
I'll make
tracks with A Tribe Called Quest and
De La Soul
sometimes I lose control when I hear the Fat Boys
make some noise for Digital Underground.
Hip Hop he sound good
in Dolby Surround Sound
or from boom boxes on street corners or on wax.
My man Hip Hop got nine lives 'cause he keep reinventing
himself.
Despite all our ups and downs together
I refuse to be a fair-weather
friend to him
'cause he be me and I be him in all his iced out glory
sometime he be the antagonist in our love story.
He never bores me
his words console me and restore my belief
that the streets breed roses from concrete.

So like Musiq for better or for worst
I'll always choose him first
'cause Hip Hop
I'll always love you.

4.24.03

Detroit Love

Rough, rugged, raw and in your face.
Pure and unadulterated
like raw sugar.
Like the first time
you got your cherry popped.
Uncut, uncensored, addictive
dressed to sweat.
Your very first poem.
Never saw it coming
defiant
start smelling yourself.
Urban, neo-soul, classic hip hop
Got a jones for 2 a.m.
taps on shoulder.
Gut wrenching
I told you so
unmistakable, undeniable
it ain't over 'till it's over
it is what it is.
Knobby kneed, pig tailed, hide and go get it,
Little Sally Walker
making mud pies on summer scorched concrete
playin' 'til the street lights come on
Sunday dinner
smellin' like church
feelin' like Aretha
testifyin'
been to the mountain top
walked through the valley of the shadow of death
can always come back home
know you're not in
Kansas anymore
'til death do us part
it all makes sense at the end of the day kinda love.

That's Detroit Love.

2.1.06

Best Supporting Actress

• A Monologue for My Future Husband

I hide behind silence/'cause when I talk/I move mountains/'cause I really can't stand clutter/and unnecessary people and things/who like to rent space out of my head/I am Black Tea/brewing with sweetened passion/wishing to be sipped slowly/I am an enigma/afraid to solve myself/'cause in real life I might start believing that I really got it going on/I am a portrait of ruby red kisses, sapphire blue dreams, emerald green moments, pink diamond mysteries/yet I settle to hide behind a water color-paint-by-number imitation of me painted by someone else/I am afraid of my past/ because it reminds me/of how worthy I really am/I am afraid to say so much/'cause I don't like being misunderstood/or not understood/or lied to/or thought to be too emotional (of which I really am)/or thought to be a contradiction/so I choose to write/and act my life out with ink/and let the paper be my stage/and the words my characters/and one day/in my real life drama/my audience of One/will give me a standing ovation/and He will whisper in my ear rave reviews/ and temper this Black Tea with honey and lemon/and sip me slowly/and watch me over and over and over again/knowing every line of my life/and love me just the same

5.16.07

Giving Birth

I want to become a woman
Who gives birth unto myself.
I want to be delicious
a caramel aphrodisiac
Sl-ow-ly melting into me.
I want to give better eargasms
and receive some extra good
lovin' with the lights on.
I want to grow more into myself.
I want to speak silence and be understood.
I want my love to produce some serious out-of-body
experiences.
I want to see myself outside in and sip cappuccino to my
greatness.
I want my femininity to be a verb, not a noun:
a state of passionate action.
I want to indulge in THIS woman's work
dividing myself into myself.
I want to be a Woman
giving birth unto myself.

3.23.01

Wisdom

Momma never told me that loving would be so exhausting
She just said don't fall in love.
Momma never said that nighttime could be so cruel, 'cause
that's usually when they leave.
That morning is much sweeter when you wake up together,
embraced.
She just said when you make your bed you have to lie in it
but she never said I could change the sheets.
Momma never told me that the best thing a father can do for
a child is to love its mother
I got that from a bookmark.
She just said a father is just a vague way to describe a man.
Momma never told me that loving a man and believing in a
man essentially means that
sometimes a man don't need no advice, just silent
acquiescence,
just a woman acknowledging that he is capable of being a
Man.
She just said don't depend on *nobody*, especially not no Man.
Momma only told me the don'ts of the man/woman thang,
but it was a *Man* who showed me the dos.
So I guess Momma was right about one thing:
loving a Man is like loving yourself, only it's the *next* best
thing.

4.20.2000

Interlude:

"Cause when you love somebody hard then you'll love that
way for life
You got all of my heart and I'll never leave your side
I gave my word to love you all the way to the end
So no matter what I'll be right here
I'll be right here 'cause we got hood love."

• **Mary J. Blige, "Hood Love"**

Love Is

Love is not a fairytale
It's not Snow White happily-ever-after-endings
and Cinderella
with her Prince Charming
I got mad loot so let me take you out the hood
classic tales of Pulp Fiction.
But what love is about
is discovering what's missing while in the kitchen
cooking for your man 'cause he's had a hard day.

It's about lonely nights and swallowing your pride 'cause he's
trying to hold it down and keep the Fam together.
So you weather your own personal storms 'cause love is more
than just about you
it's about us.
So you prioritize your needs and plant your seeds so you two
in the future can shine together

'cause love is a hustle
a steady grind of keeping your mind on what's important and
brushing the shallow nonsense off your shoulders and not
letting the past undermine the present every time he shows
up when you know you've shown out.
That's what love is all about.

It's about: real talk, the real deal, and real life in real time,
not a fairytale reflection of bed time stories about knights in
shining armor.
Just 2 beings becoming one flesh
doing the best with what they have
which is each other.

12.31.06

Untitled

You can't tell me that people have thrown rocks at me and
hid their hands.
You can't tell me that like David I've destroyed Goliaths with
my faith.
You can't tell me that I've had to cut the grass to see the
snakes.

You can't tell me I've been bitten by the ones with the
venom on their tongues.
You can't tell me that I've haven't been hung out to dry, but
like Lazarus I rise.
You can't tell me you've seen the world through my eyes or
overcome obstacles in my size nines.

You can't tell me that I won't shine even in the dark.
You can't tell me that I haven't been betrayed 'cause Peter
denied Jesus.
You can't tell me God won't provide Exodus from my fears
because He did it for Moses.

You can't tell me that every closed eye is sleep.
You can't tell me that doors otherwise closed won't be open
for me.
You can't tell me that the turtle won't catch up with the
rabbit eventually.

You see there is nothing you can say or do to alter my
reality.
No use trying to convince me that I've struggled in vain
'cause the deeper the pain the greater the destiny
and mine is yet fulfilled.

8.13.05

I Can Only Be Me - A Celebration Poem

I remember playing hide-n-go-seek on the block.
Playing 21 on the block and pick-em-up-mess-em-up on the
block
and double dutch on the block
and being fast with the Fam on the block.
Just a skinny girl with a press n curl
whose world
was filled with penny candy
and playin' 'til the street lights came on.
I was just plain Dee Dee
growin' up on the West Side of the D

until I got knocked off my square
and became a quick tempered rose growing in concrete.
A billboard for low self-esteem
selling my body for the bling
confused bed springs with heart strings.
I became a Runaway Love
an unheard of,
Gossip.
Talked about in hushed tones
tried to dethrone this diamond
into a rhinestone
said I would never be more than unknown.
That I would fold like laundry
and so I became a refugee
from my own life.

But one day I stopped running
and started standing.
I stopped running
and started standing.
I stopped running
and started standing on my pain and realized that my
mistakes made me great.

And I started to see the real ones from the fake
cut the grass to see the snakes
could see beyond the smiles
and taste
the venom on their tongues.
They thought that I would become undone
but no weapon formed against me prospered
for He brought me through and held me down.
G-O-D.
Now my haters envy me
stalkin' me like paparazzi.
Thought they had me cornered
mistook me for an amateur.
Somebody should have warned
the haters to guard their grill
'cause Love is always the last woman standing
and her name is Dee Dee.
A living testimony
of the last being the first
overcoming the hurt
overcoming the naysayers
overcoming the backstabbers
overcoming the jealousy.
Overcoming the hate, the anger, the wannabes
I guess your momma never told you every closed eye ain't
sleep.

So take a good look at me
'cause I may not be what you want me to be
but I'm what I'm suppose to be.
So you can either hate it or love it.
You can either take all of me or walk away empty handed
'cause in real life it feels really good to be just plain Dee
Dee
a skinny girl with a press n curl from the West Side of the D.

2.25.07

35

Thought Process

I want to:
Inhale your thoughts
Exhale your thoughts
Dream your thoughts
And wake up in the Garden of Eden.

I want to:
Follow your thoughts
Think your thoughts
See your thoughts
Pray your thoughts
Praise your thoughts
Give birth to your thoughts
and reproduce more of YOU.

I want to:
Feed on your thoughts
Chew on your thoughts
Drink your thoughts
and talk about your thoughts over candlelight.

I want to:
Touch your thoughts
Taste your thoughts
Feel your thoughts
Hear your thoughts
Smell your thoughts
Make your thoughts my sixth sense.

I want to:
Get full off your thoughts
Drown in your thoughts
Be fire baptized in your thoughts
Speak your thoughts
Remember your thoughts.

Wear your thoughts on my sleeve
Resurrect your thoughts in times of need
Stand on your thoughts in time of victory
Release your thoughts when I'm broken – hearted.

I want to:
Spray on your thoughts like my favorite perfume
and let your thoughts linger on my skin.
I want to capture your thoughts
Tweet you thoughts
Update my status with your thoughts
Take my time with your thoughts
Give shout-outs to your thoughts
Rock stages with your thoughts
Deliver with your thoughts
Make Sunday dinner with your thoughts.

I want to:
Worship you with your thoughts
Work your thoughts
Cater to your thoughts
Model your thoughts like FancyModelFlo in six inch heels.
Make use of your thoughts
have a that's what's up moment with your thoughts
awaken my taste buds with your thoughts.

I want to:
Color outside the lines with your thoughts
Play hide and I go seek with your thoughts
Become sand box buddies with your thoughts.

I want to:
Write choir music with your thoughts
Be an open book of your thoughts
Search for your thoughts and
Discover your thoughts like a Word Search.
Bleed your thoughts

and give transfusions to the sick.
Write haikus with your thoughts
Speak your thoughts in sign language
and give interpretations.
Take flight with your thoughts
Walk in your thoughts and
Roll deep with my home girls Goodness and Mercy.

But, most importantly,
God in your thoughts
I want to discover myself while releasing
You.

10.25.2010

Disc Three: Rhymes

All I Really Want for Christmas

All I really want for Christmas
is the rebirth of Aaliyah
Left Eye
June Jordan
Gwendolyn Brooks
Tupac
Biggie
Sam
And Jam Master Jay.
Give Malcolm X his own
holiday.
Have Spike Lee write a screenplay based on gossip and call it
"Nosy People Get It Too."
All I really want for Christmas.

All I really want for Christmas
is for these old cats to stop actin' like we a generation lost
when you gave us the directions
misconceptions
you named Roe vs. Wade.
Took our fetal brains on Mary Jane trips
it's time to skip the ego trips
and take ownership and desist with the nonsense
that age is a sense of entitlement.
All I really want for Christmas.

All I really want for Christmas is for Nas to rule the world
for someone to impregnate me with Langston Hughes' seed
so that I can give birth to music and call her Brown Sugar
and sing to her LL Cool J lullabies and read her Slick Rick
fairy tales.

Post bail for all my political prisoners
have dinner with Sonia
Nikki

Jessica
Zora
Toni
and call it "The Last Supper."
All I really want for Christmas.

All I really want for Christmas
is for Kwame to become President and Mos Def to write the
National Anthem.
For the Black Panthers to finally be recognized as the
original
Men In Black.
All I really want for Christmas.

All I really want for Christmas
is for my sistas to find peace of mind without giving up the
behind.
To feel good on the inside before they make him feel good
on the outside.
For mothers to stop telling us daughters how it should be and
start telling us how it is.
To stop having grandma raise your kids when obviously she
didn't do to great a job with you.
All I really want for Christmas.

All I really want for Christmas
is for jealousy and envy to be replaced with reciprocity and
humanity.
To engage in less retrospect and disrespect and more
introspection of the skeletons in our closets.
All I really want for Christmas.

All I really want for Christmas
is the ending of all self-imposed limitations
the cessation
of these get quick sensations that produce illegitimate
babies,

'Bling Bling' dynasties,
and the extinction of the black family.
All I really want for Christmas.

All I really want for Christmas
is for someone to tell my people how beautiful that they be
is for someone to tell my people how beautiful that they be
and just maybe, if we believe it hard enough we'll be free.

All I really want for Christmas...

12.3.02

Black Thought

I bleed Black blood from a Black heart wounded by Black people
so I cry Black tears from a Black soul seeking redemption
from a Black God who plants Black seeds in my Black mind
to sow with my Black hands.
Generations of Black pearls and Black diamonds
fathom impossibilities
in the Blackest night while being Blackmailed by a system
that capitalizes on Black skin and Black inventions and who
pimp the Black wish of my forefathers whose Black power
runs through me like still waters.

I'm watched by Black angels who spin Black magic inside
of Black ink wells so that I, a Black woman can preserve
my legacy in Black ink and speak in my Black tongue the
language of the speechless
and find rest in knowing that my Black English can impart
Black power to little Black birds whose wings have been
clipped like coupons.
Whose saved souls have been lost and never found and
although I sometime stand on shaky ground
I know I am held by Black hands and stand tall and proud
on Black shoulders knowing that I am a Black woman whose
only hurdle is herself.

5.22.05

44

I Knew You Was a Real Poet

I knew you was a real poet 'cause it was like game recognizing
game.
When I spoke my name and you spoke yours,
it was like the way Coltrane did a Love Supreme.
I guess things ain't always what they seem.
Who knew a kid nicknamed "Bullet" who rocks baggy jeans
would have teenagers addicted to by-lines like fiends.
I mean
I knew you was a real poet.

I mean you pen revolutionary ballads like Miles Davis did jazz
I mean brother you bad
how you prophesy street dreams on notepads.
I wish I had pennies for your thoughts
'cause I be rich.
Is it magic the way you flip that ghetto Sanskrit
or is just God's gift that you emit?

I mean
I knew you was a real poet
'cause I saw fit to pen you a classic fit for a king
immortalize you with similes
do lyrical battles with your adversaries.

It's scary how the pen is mightier than the sword.

So, DeAntjuan
keep building nations
with your words.
DeAntjuan
stir revolutions with your pen.
DeAntjuan
write freedom songs with your words
and DeAntjuan despite what you heard
'Regular Adversaries' do go on to do big things.

5.14.2003

Real Talk

See they spoke about
you in hushed tones
as if you were gossip.
Said you never make it because of your Makavelli branded
skin
too busy comparing you to the then
never appreciating your beauty in the now.
Said you were lost and would never be found
like change in couch cushions.
But you kept pushin' like roots
through concrete.
They tried to silence you when you speak
'cause you remind them of what they should've been as
parents, as teachers, as adults so they tired to shut you up.
Said you had
smart mouths and lacked r-e-s-p-e-c-t
but they never tried to see
that you are a reflection of us and sometimes narcissism can
be painful.

See they turned their noses
up to your 9 to 5
and your 6 to 10
under the table hustle.
Yet they
told you to stop being lazy and to get your own so you did
but it still wasn't enough.
So you said forget it and tatted
"Thug Life"
on your hearts
and corn rowed your souls and put
Apples on your Bottoms
in hopes that you would be picked daily by young soldiers
who wore rose colored chains around their necks to
compensate for the roses daddy never sent.

46

Yet, you never let anyone rent space out of your head.
Got by
by any means necessary even if it meant flippin' that money
three ways. For that I thank you 'cause without you I would
be speechless with no words to recite.
It's because of you I write.
It's because of you I know that it'll never rain 40 days and 40
nights.
With you it's never might.

You are blessings,
the voice of the poems I ain't even written yet.

So I speak the realest words I ever wrote to tell you:
Never let them label you as setbacks,
write you off
like a bad debt.
And don't worry
about others sleepin' on you
'cause as long as they keep sleepin'
you can keep dreamin'
and that's real.

6.5.2005

I Spy

I am a Poet.
I do not make the rules or tell the reader what to feel.
I just pen miniseries that are microscopes of your daily
existence.

I am a Peeping Tom who can artistically paint your life
from A-Z and cleverly disguise your imperfections with
metaphorical face paint leaving you to say: 'that was deep.'
Too deep for you to recognize that a perfect stranger sized
you up like a McDonald's value meal
in the time it will take you to read this line in the book you
call your life written by a Ghost Writer moonlighting as a
Poet
who only writes what she is told and who doesn't ask
questions.

I just tell your story the way it should be lived.

7.24.09

The Process

Six months I dreamed in color.
Waited, compromised, searched outside
myself for my pot of goal at the end of my rainbow.
I stood briefly on the sidelines and watched others
live aimlessly, sometimes recklessly in an oil painting created
by others.
Never choosing their own colors, or background or strokes
just still lives in the moment drying permanently on
someone else's canvas yet calling it their paint-by-number
life.
Hiding, running from the slip of the Artist's hand trying to
avoid
colors that attempted to paint outside the lines and spill
bleeding, diluted shades into my picture.
For six months I've dodged the Artist who tired to paint my
life.
For six months I darkened the outlines of my painting to
distinguish my portrait from others.
For six months I blended shades to create brighter hues and
broaden my strokes to create larger than life moments and
created a Masterpiece
to be hung slightly off balance
by choice.

8.6.2000

I Apologize for Not Being a Rapper...

Welcome ladies and gentlemen!
Tonight for your listening pleasure
We've got DJ Langston Hughes
Mic check, one two, one two.
Lady Nikki Giovanni will be your M.C.
Mic check, one two, one two.
And then there's me...
Mic check, one two, one two.

I apologize for not being a rapper...

Instead I spit haikus, sonnets, and love verses
minus dress rehearsals
my metaphors are universal.
'Cause a rose is still as sweet
when coupled with an iambic pentameter beat.

Sorry I don't make you dance in your seat
but instead I cause you to retreat
into yellows and Mo Betta Blues.
You see I give you food,
food for thought
letting you get caught
in my web of verbal reverse psychology.
As I catch you moving to the beat of my similes
'cause I'm discreet
with my rhythms
sign, sealed, and delivered.
By the time you catch on
millions of words have been born
and are now traveling to the honeycomb spaces between
your ears.

I apologize for not being a rapper...

Sorry but there's no hook to make your head nod
no R & B singer
to add artificial sweeteners
to my remix.
Dick Clark and 106 and Park
won't give me shout-outs
but my words set sparks after dark.

An aphrodisiac for two
or maybe an after dinner mint for three.
I guess I'm too HIP to HOPscotch on the Grammy's
'cause my poetry
doesn't fit MTV.
Sounds much better when DJ Hughes spins it on wax
than your DVD and MP3's

'cause my words come in Dolby Surround Sound Stereo
my meters provide Sony style acoustics.
I can take you on trips
to Rome, Africa, Italy, Harlem
in just one syllable.
Give you eargasms with A-E-I-O-U
and sometimes drop a bass line with Y.
My lyrics fly
and soar 360°
to the honeycomb spaces between your ears.

I apologize for not being a rapper
Mic check, one two, one two...
Goodnight y'all.

7.2.2002

51

If I Only Had Five Minutes – The Last Will and Testament of a Hip Hop Poet

If I only had five minutes
I would resurrect the Harlem Renaissance Poets
lead a lyrical insurrection
like Nat Turner
become a Poetical Head Hunter
engage in some serious Slam Session orgies
impregnate my creative seed
and give birth to Black Ink (wells) who
create revolutionary ballads on white paper.
If I only had five minutes.

If I only had five minutes
I would write a mad love poem for my little
Soul Sistas:
Krystyna and Cenovia
Danessa and Dominique
Jermieka and Shatika
Angelica and Annie
Qulicia and Jasia
Tricia, Lea, and LaGina
my little Soul Sistas on Dexter and Davison
Linwood and Nevada
Livernois and 7 Mile
Joy Road and Puritan
Chalmers and Hayes
engage them in creative dialogue versus premarital
monologue.
Teach them to fall in love with words instead of bodies.
Tell them to French Kiss sonnets
instead of Ciroc stained male lips.
If I only had five minutes.

If I only had five minutes

I'd write a haiku
for Lorraine Hansberry
'cause now I understand what it means to be Young, Gifted,
and Black
'cause poets all we are, are walking, talking schizophrenics
with beautiful minds who have conversations with vowels
and make dates with syllables.
If I only had five minutes.

If I only had five minutes
I'd give shout-outs to my reflections
Marlon, Emmanuel, Sean, and Anthony
Who dig me despite all my idiosyncrasies.
If I only had five minutes.

If I only had five minutes
I would like Ike Turner, five, five, five you into lyrical
submission
force-feed you my Alphabet Soup
tie you up with my metaphorical dominatrix
create an artificial matrix for spoken word and call it BET.
Pimp you and have you write me poetry.
If I only had five minutes.

If I only had five minutes
as the last Hip Hop Poet,
let it be like Claude McKay, "not like [a] hog, haunted and
penned in an inglorious spot, [but] pressed to the wall, dying
but fighting back."

If I only had five minutes.

8.2.02

53

Interlude:

"The thing about hip – hop is that it's from the underground, ideas from the underbelly, from people who have mostly been locked out, who have not been recognized."
- Russell Simmons

Closing Credits:

"You could thank me now, go 'head/Thank me later, yeah, I know what I said/But later doesn't always come so instead/ It's okay, you could thank me now."

• **Drake, "Thank Me Now"**

EXECUTIVE PRODUCER: GOD FOR DEUTERONOMY 8:18 PRODUCTIONS
CREATIVE DIRECTOR: Tia DeShay **COVER DESIGN:** Thinkstock (www.thinkstockphotos.com), AuthorHouse (www.authorhouse.com), Team Tiber, Tia DeShay
INTERIOR PHOTOGRAPHY: Tia DeShay
FAN MAIL:
Facebook: @DeeAV
Twitter: @TiaDeShay
Blogger: www.handpickedhelpingadoptees.blogspot.com
Email: averhart20@aol.com
PHOTOGRAPHY (Back Cover): Daryl Burgess
HAIR: Gen of Hair Entourage Salon, Detroit, Michigan
MAKE-UP: Tia DeShay
SUPPORT TEAM: Averharts, Halls, Maloneys, Hoods, McGhees, Boswells, Leonards, & Feazell – Bests, Larry "DJ L Boog" Phillips, Lynn Shaw of Red V Events Planning, Family Victory Fellowship, Ty Lamar & Eva Miller